POMPOSA

History and art of Abbey

Written by:
CARLA DI FRANCESCO

Published by
ITALCARDS
bologna Italy

Distributore esclusivo
ADG

Historical background

The settlement of Benedictine monks in Pomposa has uncertain origins, even though there are enough reasons to believe that a monastic community already lived there in the 7th century. The first document mentioning the Abbey *, however, dates back to the year 874. It tells about one of the many disputes arisen over the centuries because of the sovereignity to which the Abbey was subject. Pope John the Eight certifies in the document that the «Monasterium Sanctae Mariae in Comaclo, qui Pomposia dicitur» and it comes within the jurisdiction of Rome, not being a dependency of the Bishop of Ravenna. In this way Pomposa enters the historical records through one of the controversial matters which were peculiar to its existence before the year 1001, when emperor Otto the Third sanctioned its independence and declared it «royal». Doubtless, the origin of the claims between Rome and Ravenna — meanwhile, in 982, emperor Otto the Third had given Pomposa to the monastery of St. Salvatore in Pavia — is to be found not only in the Abbey's cultural and spiritual greatness but also in the economic stability which the Abbey had reached as a result of a particularly favourable geographical position. In fact, «insula Pomposia», was relatively close to one

of the most important routes to Rome (the ancient «Via Popilia», which came to be called «Romea» in the Middle Ages because it used to lead pilgrims coming from north-eastern Europe to the Holy City), but at the same time it was formed by two main branches of the Po delta, the Volano-Po to the south and the Gauro, or Goro-Po, to the north, which represented a strong advantage for trade and river navigation. Its nearness to the Adriatic Sea, from which it was separated by the delta lagoon, had good effects on climate, very healthy, and on flourishing farming activities: fields under cultivation and the saline of Comacchio are reported as part of the Abbey's estate in the 10th century.

During the following centuries donations and bequests of territories scattered all over Italy added wealth to the already good economic situation of the Abbey: the new possessions, in regions like Veneto, Umbria, even in Piedmont etc., increased sensibly the Abbey's power which reached the apex of its expansion in the second half of the 11th century. That was the time of the Monastery's economic splendour: after being declared independent, in 1001, it became a cultural, spiritual and artistic centre of a very high level and welcoming

personalities such as San Pier Damiani and Guido d'Arezzo and abbots of remarkably strong personalities like St. Guido and Mainardo.

The Abbey was enlarged to lodge the over one hundred monks living there in the 11th century. A cloister *, now destroyed, was built and around it were the places corresponding to the different moments of monks'community and working life: a capitular hall, a refectory, a guest-room, a library and a dormitory. The building complex is supposed having been integrated by other secondary buildings connected to manual labour and productive activities in general.

Still nowadays the Court-house gives proof of the fact that abbots administered justice in the territories within were subject to their jurisdiction, organized on a feudal basis, retaining however a direct power upon the populations of the «insula Pomposia» and of Codigoro. Closely related as it was to a particularly favourable position, the prosperity of Pomposa began to decline when, in 1152, the breach of the Po at Ficarolo started a slow but steady process which eventually changed the geographic profile of the delta. It was in fact a tremendous flood, followed by a northward shifting of the main river branches and by a gradual turning into marshland of the Pomposa lagoon area.

The geographic change was of course a matter of centuries, so much that in the 14th century the Abbey was still thriving and growing rich in new artistic works. But the impoverishment of soil and malaria were already present at the end of the 12th century: in 1235 the Abbey totalled 20 monks while in 1306 they were only 10.

At the beginning of the 15th century the Abbey was given in commendam, that is to say it was assigned to a commendatory Abbot external to the community. At the end of the century it was put under the dependency of the new monastery of St. Benedict in Ferrara to which were moved, in a few decades, the possessions of Pomposa, consisting of works of art, pieces of furniture, the archive, the library, etc. In 1653 Pope Innocent the Tenth decreed the formal dissolution of the monastic institution which the last monks left in 1671. From then on decay and neglect came to be an integral part of all the events the abbatial buildings were

---

* Words marked by an asterisk are explained in alphabetical order in the glossary on page 95.

Pomposa and the surrounding area: the bell-tower is a very important landmark.

3

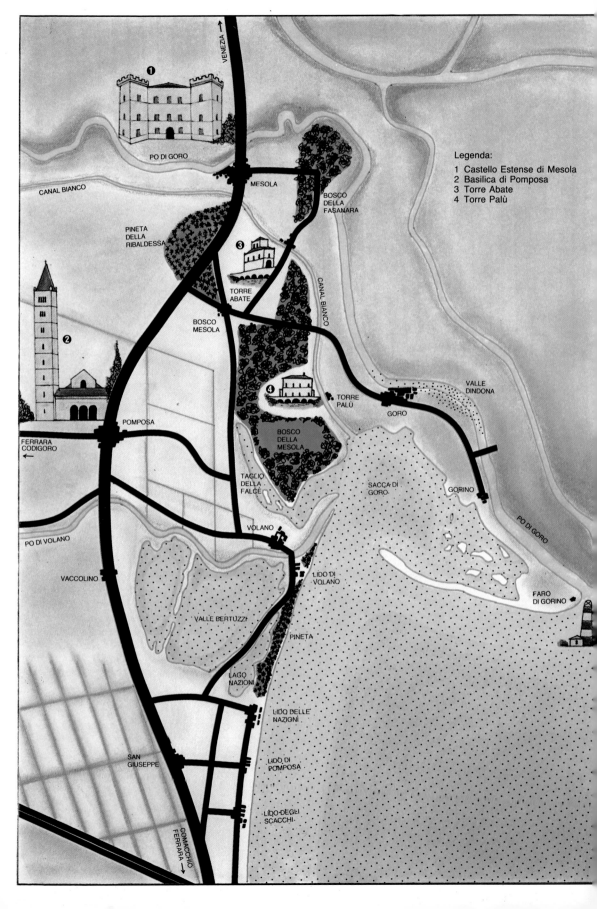

VENEZIA

PO DI GORO

CANAL BIANCO

MESOLA

BOSCO
DELLA
FASANARA

PINETA
DELLA
RIBALDESSA

Legenda:
1 Castello Estense di Mesola
2 Basilica di Pomposa
3 Torre Abate
4 Torre Palù

TORRE
ABATE

BOSCO
MESOLA

CANAL BIANCO

VALLE
DINDONA

TORRE
PALÙ

GORO

POMPOSA

FERRARA
CODIGORO
←

BOSCO
DELLA
MESOLA

SACCA DI
GORO

GORINO

TAGLIO
DELLA
FALCE

PO DI GORO

PO DI VOLANO

VOLANO

VACCOLINO

LIDO DI
VOLANO

FARO
DI GORINO

VALLE BERTUZZI

PINETA

LAGO
NAZIONI

LIDO DELLE
NAZIONI

SAN
GIUSEPPE

LIDO DI
POMPOSA

LIDO DEGLI
SCACCHI

COMACCHIO
FERRARA
→

to pass through: the Napoleonic suppressions, the sale to the Guiccioli family (1802), the use of the buildings for the owner's farming activities.

When the Abbey became State property, preservation works were initiated to avoid further falls and destructions of the buildings and then to recover the architectural and artistic works as well as the prestigious painting cycles contained in them. Though far from being concluded, this preservation action is at least arrived to an advanced stage. Again, environmental conditions have favourably influenced the «renaissance» of Pomposa: beginning from the second half of the last century, reclaiming activities have turned marsh into arable land and eradicated malaria, thus removing the isolation to which the Abbey had been sentenced by the breach of Ficarolo.

1. The Abbey towards south, seen from the bell-tower: in the left block of the building there are the capitular hall, the hall of the boards and the dormitory (today a museum); on the opposite side there is the refectory. 2. A view of the court-house. On pages 6-7 a view of the Pomposa building complex.

St. Guido and the personalities of Pomposa

The most outstanding personality among all the ones connected to the name of Pomposa is Abbot St. Guido, of the Strambiati family from Ravenna. He died in 1046 after a forty years' enlightened leadership of the Monastery. A wise administrator and a well-balanced religious, he was able to obtain possessions and privileges from the Roman Curia, and he devoted himself to the enlargement of the church, thereby leading the Abbey to its most splendid period of prosperity and power.

He was cleverly engaged in religious matters too, and he gave hospitality to St. Pier Damiani from 1040 to 1042, so that he could teach the monks. Pomposa became therefore one of the most important centres of spirituality and a religious point of reference at a time when Church was tottering under the heavy burden of simony and waiting for new contributions to renew effectively its structure.

Having died away from Pomposa, St. Guido was buried at first in Verona, in the St. Zeno Church, and his mortal remains were later on moved to Spina by emperor Henry the Third, where they became the object of deep reverence.

Under Abbot St. Guido Pomposa entered into relations with several powerful persons and reli-

2

gious men: among them, besides emperor Otto the Third who declared its independence, are Marquis Bonifacio di Canossa, the father of Matilde, who was «converted» by St. Guido to a life more linked to Christian ideals, and Gebeardo, the Bishop of Ravenna. In his presence the Saint performed the miracle which was later painted in fresco in the refectory: convinced of the holiness of monastic life, Gebeardo wanted to be buried in Pomposa.

The culture of Pomposa in that fertile period is also enlightened by the presence of Guido d'Arezzo, a monk who was also a revolutionary innovator in the field of music: after entering the Monastery at a very early age, there Guido «invented» the musical writing, i.e. the same system of staff and notes at regular intervals which is still used nowadays as an instrument of universal understanding of music.

1

1. Abbot St. Guido, a detail of the capitular hall fresco. 2. The miracle of St. Guido, a detail of the refectory fresco. 3. The abbatial church of St. Mary.

The church

History of its construction

If we consider the state of mutilation of the remaining buildings complex, the Abbey of St. Mary is undoubtedly the most remarkable element of the whole group of edifices in Pomposa. Above all, however, the Abbey represents a unique «piece» of art because of its very high architectural, decorative and pictorial quality, a basic reference in the history of art as a pattern of the Romanesque architecture of the Po Valley. It is one of those monuments which are not deprived in any way of importance and charm in spite of partial defacements, changes and replacements, however serious and painful these may have been.

Today the sight of the façade conveys an effect which is very different from the one offered by the Abbey up to a few decades ago, when the avenue, lined with Italian poplars, and small cypresses framed the atrium * from the distance thus letting it appear or rather be discovered gradually, as vi-

sitors approached. Until that time there were neither asphalted roads nor parkings or gardens around the Abbey: the bell tower revealed from far away the presence of the Monument rising amidst cultivated fields. This was of course a picture from the 19th century, a romantic image which nevertheless used to give the idea of an old nobility which had survived decline, malaria and misfortune owing to its intrinsic and real greatness.

Therefore, the old suggestive sight is now dampened by an environment «tamed» by the presence of a man who altered it to meet his present needs. Nonetheless, the encounter with the atrium, only apparently simple, and with the bell tower, at the same time massive and lightened by refined decorations, is still able to arouse a strong emotion.

Scholars agree to date the first church in Pomposa to the 8th century: it had a basilican plan * with a nave * and two aisles *, each one having a Ravenna-like apse (semicircular inside and polygonal outside) and it was preceded by a portico with a double span covered by vaults. This structure was preserved through all subsequent changes and is partly recognizable by traces of walled-up, two-light * windows in the interior.

The church was enlarged to its present size under St. Guido: the old atrium was sacrificed to allow an extension of the plan, thereby adding two more spans to the previous seven, of which the more recent are wider than the older ones bringing more light. Reconstructed, decorated with frescoes and rich mosaic * and inlaid marble floors, the church was consecrated in 1026. Not much later, still in the first half of the 11th century, the atrium was built by maestro Mazulo, as is reported by an inscription on the façade (the variant «Mazulone» has been just recently suggested); according to tradition the master was born in Ravenna.

During the second half of the 11th century, in

South side of the church and bell-tower: in the foreground one of the cloister angular pillars.

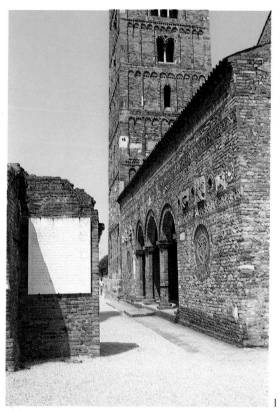

1063, another event of basic importance for the architectural history of the St. Mary basilica occurred: the foundation of the bell tower, a work by an artist called, in the dedicatory stone, Deusdedit.

At the end of the century the church had then reached its present shape, with the exception of the two side apses which were built in 1150. Information about these works as well as their year of execution are reported on the stone which lies to the left of the atrium's façade, on which is given also the name of the abbot who fostered the work, John of Vidor.

Another meaningful date for the artistic history of Pomposa is the year 1351, when the frescoes * in the apse, attributed to Vitale da Bologna, were begun; about twenty years later the church walls had frescoes painted again on previous decorations: it was the completion of one of the most thorough and suggestive sacred painting cycle of the 14th century.

Apart from the removal of the south apse, suppressed in the 14th century for functional reasons, no remarkable events are recorded in the church history until, in the 19th century, it was decided to save it from collapse by completing the seven supporting walls which interrupt the atrium in three parts and the aisles at each span. As a result, the interior unfortunately took up a completely different aspect which makes it unrecognizable to anyone who tries to understand its simple, basilican space as essence of regular and continuous rhythm stressed by dot-like supports.

After that, only restorations aimed at the preservation of the existing monuments occurred in this century.

It is advisable to begin a visit to what remains of the Abbey with the church itself, lingering over the atrium and the bell tower and then going inside the Museum of Pomposa; downstairs the visit continues into the capitular hall, the refectory and finally into the Court-house.

1. A foreshortening of the entrance-hall. 2. The ruins of the main body west of the cloister with the memorial stone reminding of the Pomposa millenary history. 3. The church façade.

The façade

The architectural forms of the atrium and the façade are of the highest simplicity: the façade's upper part, with a simple sloping roof, is punctuated by two windows with one opening *, the only apertures in the bare surface of the wall. In the foreground we see the atrium, consisting of a solid brickwork emptied in the middle by the openings of three arches which represent the entrance to the church, and lightened, at the sides of the said arches, by two circular pierced barriers *.

Though prevailing, the brickwork surface is far from being massive: the chromatic play of red and yellow bricks, the carved brickworks and the maiolica and stone decorations contribute to create a unique whole, so different from the coeval buildings and so enigmatic to allow a number of hypothesis and doubts about its origin to be put forward by scholars and experts.

This atrium in fact represents one of the most fascinating episodes of the artistic history of the Po Valley, not so much for the form of the composition, which draws inspiration from traditional patterns, as for the originality of the decorations, all aimed at highlighting the valuable particulars of the surface, both through the warm playing of the two colours and through the refined ornamentation of the reliefs which cover it in parallel series and again through single decorative elements.

It is worth adding some remarks about the atrium just because, as mentioned above, it is of extraordinary historical interest, particularly as far as decorations are concerned. As a matter of fact, all scholars seem to agree that this decoration series is to be attributed to an oriental culture in general, although each theme has a more precise connotation: as for the two round barriers made of stucco *, for example, the oriental inspiration is shown by an iconography of Persian origin in which two winged gryphons eat fruits from a central tree representing the tree of life; most probably the image spread into the West through the trade of decorated cloth. Moreover, in the ribbon-like edge of brickwork which surrounds the barriers, interesting comparisons with architectural elements typical of the Syrian region have been recently suggested. Another trace of the oriental culture contribution has been seen in the arrangement of the decorated bands which run horizontally on the wall surface regardless of the architectural frames, as well as in the characteristic foliage bands with alternated figures and plant elements.

So, the enigma mentioned above becomes evident: the wide use of non-autochthonous stylistic elements opposed to an artificer, maestro Mazulo, allegedly born in Ravenna. It is much more

14

3

probable that the master simply lived in the Italian town but that he originally came from the other shores of the Adriatic Sea, as has been recently supposed.

The band which lies at middle height of the homogeneous portions of the wall is different from the others, being formed by maiolica basins, surrounded by a star-shaped, yellow-red edge, and evidently coeval with the façade although the bowls are of later production. Stone reliefs representing a peacock, an eagle and a lion are alternated with the basins and arranged symmetrically to the entrance. They may with good reason be regarded as more recent works.

Two important memorial stones can be seen at both sides of the spans: to the right is the one reminding of the construction of the atrium by Mazulo («I, maestro Mazulo, who have done this

1. The middle arcade of the entrance-hall: in this picture the decorative bands of two-coloured brickworks are put into special relief. 2. The right side of the entrance-hall. 3. The left side of the entrance-hall. 4. A detail of the entrance-hall: the memorial stone reminding of the works done in the church in 1150.

4

work, beg you to pray for me our Lord and say: may the Almighty have mercy upon you»); to the left, under a small spoil * Roman bust, a memorial stone coming from another building announces the works of the year 1150.

A curious particular, probably something inserted contemporaneously to the original decoration, is represented by a small head of brickwork on the right side of the façade at the same level as the first maiolica basin from the left: it is the only human figure among so many fictitious and real animals, leaves and branches, apart from the «strange» figure, perhaps a friar, by means of which the brickwork band over the round barriers rests on the right span of the portico.

---

1. A detail of the entrance-hall: a brickwork griffin overhanging the left arch. 2. A detail of the entrance-hall: a relief of a peacock between two ceramic basins. 3. A detail of the entrance-hall: a circular stucco «transenna» with winged griffins and a brick-work, ribbonlike band. On the left the memorial stone reminding of Mazulo's work. 4. A detail of the entrance-hall: the lion of the left wall with a majolica basin.

The bell tower

If the decorations of the Pomposa atrium influenced later works of art of the whole Po Valley and the North Adriatic shore (from Venice to Bologna etc.), they were of course not unknown to maestro Deusdedit, the builder of the bell tower.

Man of ideas completely different from Mazulo's, who surely in the field of architecture had not been much of an innovator, Deusdedit carried out a work of remarkable modernity connected with the most advanced achievements of the Lombardic-Romanesque style.

After all, the time of the tower's construction (the reference reported by the memorial stone at the basis of the building is the year 1063) was in Italy the period of the flourishing of the Romanesque architecture and Deusdedit shows therefore to be deeply rooted in the culture of his own time. To the same extent to which the atrium still retains elements of doubt and mistery, because of the far-reaching antecedents mentioned

1. A view of the bell-tower. 2. The bell-tower, a detail of one of the mullioned windows. 3. The bell-tower towards east: in the foreground the polygonal church apse and the left little apse.

1

above, the bell tower on the contrary presents itself quite openly and fits easily into a specific, autochthonous culture.

The huge structure which rises over the surrounding area starts on the ground with a massive stone base and continues upwards with a brick wall broken by windows with one opening of increasing width up to the fourth level; from there on, apertures (two-, three *- and four-light windows *) become wider and wider until, in the belfry, walls are almost non-existent; the tower is crowned by a conic spire * with sloping bricks.

The arrangement of masses, related to the strong contrast of empty and full volumes, and the theme of spaces interrupted by small arches and pilaster strips * enhances the plastic value of the whole in a typical Romanesque style. Walls are made more attractive by decorations similar to those of the atrium, but used together with new ones and in a more imaginative way: the frameworks of brickwork, for example, are not the same for all the floors and only one of them shows the theme of foliage and figures widely used in the atrium. Here we find again maiolica basins of oriental origin in various positions. Another peculiar feature of the bell tower is the reuse of architectural elements (capitals and columns) coming from different constructions, which gives evidence of the habit, widespread in Pomposa, of collecting parts from buildings of earlier times.

The interior

A first look into the church interior conveys the idea of a building of great homogeneity and richness, in spite of the said serious losses suffered by the lateral spaces. Here, in fact, artistic expressions of highest level coexist and, although dating back to different times, form a grandiose whole. Therefore a comprehensive visit to the church teaches us how to read the original structure, the enlargements, the adornments and the following decorations; in other words how to understand the sense of an artistic greatness which was produced over a number of centuries (from the 8th to the 14th) and saw Pomposa always in the foreground.

The simple basilican plan and the apse with a polygonal external perimeter reveal the influence of the nearby Ravenna buildings on this 8th century church; typical of the Ravenna-Byzantine style is also the linking of capital and arch by means of the pulvin *; more, the architectural elements, particularly the spoil capitals, come most likely from buildings of Ravenna and Classe.

The remains of the old atrium (two-light windows) are clearly recognizable in the two first spans beside the façade. The raised presbyterium and the crypt * below were instead rebuilt in our century during various restoration works. The floor with mosaics and marble inlays deserves particular attention. It is divided into four separate sectors: the first three of which, against the presbyterium, were once the floor of the monks' choir *, now destroyed but recognized in 1978-79 in its perimeter and shape during excavations carried out by the Monuments and Fine Arts Service of Ravenna. The choir's enclosure, made of small pillars and stucco barriers (some fragments are preserved in the Museum) is attributable to the time of the great works promoted by Abbot Guido as is reported by a date on one of the arms of the cross in the central panel: 7 May 1026.

The first sector of the floor is doubtless one of the many pieces coming from Ravenna buildings and was laid there when the two remaining sectors were made: it is a mosaic floor and for its workmanship and design may be dated to the 6th century.

The second sector has inlays with polychrome marbles and in its centre lies a circle from which the four arms of a cross branch off. The decoration, in concentric circles, is bordered by a band forming four smaller circles at the corners of the square into which it is inscribed.

The mosaic of the following panel has themes and forms from the Middle Ages; poor-quality animals fill the spaces limited by badly intertwined bands.

The fourth sector, about a century more recent than the others, is a very refined work of precious

1. A foreshortening of the bell-tower. 2. The church's interior. 3. The church, third sector of the floor: a detail of the animal in the central panel.

21

1. The church, third sector of the floor: details of animals on the edge band and of the central picture. 2. The church - a view of the floor near the apse: above, the mosaic sector of the 6th century; in the middle, the inlaid panel (1026); below the animals' sector.

23

1

marbles. Unfortunately missing in the part adjoining the façade and extensively restored in our century, it must have been a big rectangle having a circle in its centre to which four smaller circles are tangent. The remaining spaces are divided into smaller squares and rectangles containing various drawings, interlaced ribbons, white fields and geometrical elements.

It is unconceivable to leave the church without spending some time to visit the frescoes * displayed on all its walls.

The part which is universally acknowledged as the most important, from a qualitative point of view, is the apse bowl-shaped vault, attributed to Vitale da Bologna; in it the blessing God inside a mandorla is surrounded by saints and angels while, on his right, Our Lady in the Virgins' choir can be

1. The church, a detail of the marble-inlaid pavement (12th century). 2. The church: a view of the inlaid pavement of the 12th century.

24

2

seen together with St. Guido and Andrea, abbot in Pomposa at the time when the fresco was painted (1351).

The apse walls are also completely frescoed with panels arranged on three levels: the upper one shows, among the windows, the figures of St. Martin and St. John the Baptist; on its sides are the Evangelists to the left and the Doctors of the Church sitting at a desk to the right.

With lively narrative inspiration the life of St. Eustachio is represented on the intermediate level, although unfortunately various parts are missing. Of the seven panels, we mention the last scene which stands out among the others for its expressive liveliness: in it Eustachio is martyrized with his wife and sons inside a metal statue which is being heated up.

In the lower level we see panels with geometrical elements similar to those displayed on the aisles'walls.

---

1. The church: a comprehensive view of the apse. 2. The apse frescoes: a detail of the basin with the blessing Christ and the heavenly crowd (Vitale da Bologna 1351). 3. The apse frescoes: a detail of the St. Eustachio tales. The scene represents Placido baptized together with his relatives, receiving the name of Eustachio (half of the 14th century).

3

1. Apse frescoes on the left: in the upper band there are the evangelists, in the lower one the St. Eustachio tales; from conversion to martyrdom; from left to right: Christ's apparition (between the deer horns), the baptism, the separation from the family, St. Eustachio weeping in exile (half of the 14th century). 2. Apse frescoes on the right: in the upper band the doctors of the church, in the lower one the tales of St. Eustachio's life; the reunion with his relatives, the trial, the prison, the martyrdom in the belly of the idol, the glory (half of the 14th century). 3. Apse frescoes: a detail of the St. Eustachio's tales: the saint in prison with his wife and sons. 4. Apse frescoes: a detail of the upper band with the doctors of the church.

The fresco of the bowl-shaped vault in the left apse is of a certain interest: it represents the blessing Christ inside a mandorla between the Virgin and St. John the Baptist; to the left a very badly damaged panel representing Our Lady with Child, angels and the investing monk on his knees.

The nave's frescoes are set on two main levels where thirtynine nine scenes depict the story of the Old and New Testament in panels of various size according to the artist's expressive need; episodes taken from the Apocalypse follow one

29

As far as the exact interpretation of each scene is concerned, it is advisable to examine the existing reading suggestions and the corresponding captions.

On the counter-façade a big fresco of The Last Judgement is displayed, a usual choice in the sacred architecture of the Middle Ages, both for the painting's theme and for its position: it served as a warning for the congregation on their leaving the church. However, many observers have pointed out that the artist who painted the judgement seems to have been extremely moderate in depicting the sufferings connected with the sentence to Hell, particularly if compared to other painters of similar scenes. Here the judgement is set in a very regular arrangement, by means of six levels over which a double representation of Christ prevails: above, standing, Christ is giving his bless-

another uninterruptedly in the spaces among the arches.

The frescoes are to be read starting from that on the south wall (on the right if one looks at the altar), high up beside the big triumph arch *; the sequence continues on this band till it reaches the façade and then on the north wall, on the upper level; back to the apse, the episode succession passes again onto the south wall, lower level, and so on.

1-2. Apse frescoes: a detail of the St. Eustachio's tales; the martyrdom and the glory. 3. The church, left apse.

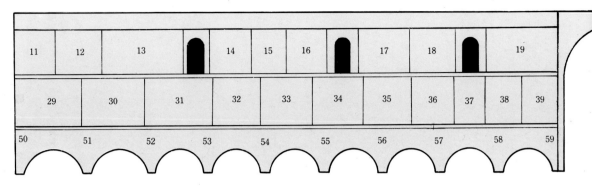

SCHEME SHOWING THE ARRANGEMENT OF FRESCOES IN THE NORTH WALL OF THE NAVE

Upper level with scenes from the Old Testament

1, Adam and Eve, stories of Cain and Abel
2, Noah's Ark
3, Abraham receives the angels
4, Abraham's hospitality
5, Isaac, Esau and Jacob
6, Jacob's dream
7, Joseph's dream and the envious brothers
8, Joseph sold to the merchants and Jacob's weeping
9, Joseph accuses Benjamin

10, Jacob blesses his sons
11,12, Unidentified scenes
13, Exodus of the Jews
14, Moses receives the Tables of the Law
15, Transportation of the Holy Ark
16, Joshua stops the sun
17, Daniel in the lions'den
18, Elijah on th chariot of fire
19, Battle

Middle level with scenes from the New Testament

20, Annunciation and Visitation
21, Nativity
22, Adoration of the Magi
23, Slaughter of the Innocents
24, Presentation to the Temple
25, Christ's baptism
26, The Marriage Feast of Cana
27, Resurrection of the rabbi's daughter
28, Resurrection of the son of Naim's widow
29, Resurrection of Lazarus

30, Entrance into Jerusalem
31, Last Supper
32, Prayer in the garden and Christ's arrest
33, Crucifixion
34, Burial in the Sepulchre
35, An Angel appears to the pious women
36, Noli me tangere (Do not touch me)
37, St. Thomas's incredulity
38, Ascension
39, Pentecost

Lower level with scenes from the Apocalypse

40, St. John Evangelist
41, The seven candelabra
42, God
43, The Lamb with the symbols of the Evangelists
44,45, The horsemen of the Apocalypse
46, Angels
47, Angel
48, An Angel offers St. John the Book
49, St. John in the temple
50, Babylon

51, Hydra threatens the Church
52, Battle between Angels and the devil
53, The seven-headed Beast
54, Angels preaching and foretelling Babylon's fall
55, The Son of Man rebukes an Angel
56, The blond prostitute
57, Riding of the Revenger and the Angels
58,59, The monster is confined to Hell

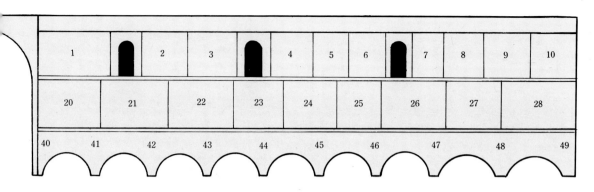

SCHEME SHOWING THE ARRANGEMENT OF FRESCOES IN THE SOUTH WALL OF THE NAVE

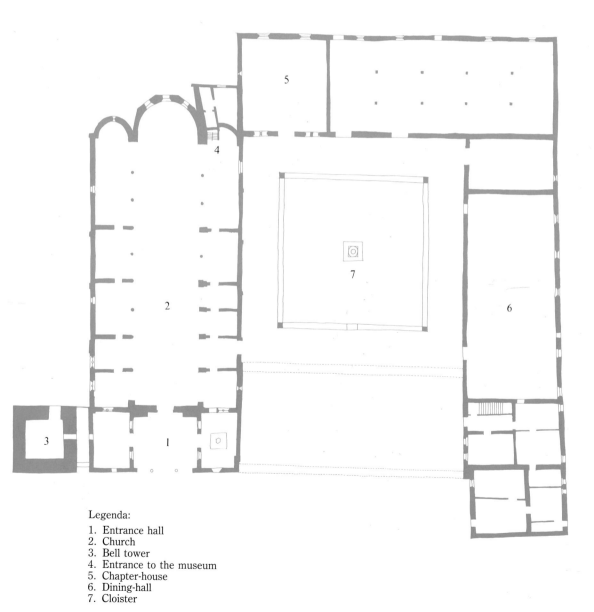

Legenda:
1. Entrance hall
2. Church
3. Bell tower
4. Entrance to the museum
5. Chapter-house
6. Dining-hall
7. Cloister

Scenes from the Old Testament

1. Nave frescoes: the Old Testament (scene 1), the sin of Adam and Eve, the tales of Cain and Abel. 2. Nave frescoes: the Old Testament (scene 3), Abraham and the angels. 3. Nave frescoes: the Old Testament (scene 4), Abraham gives hospitality to the angels. 4. Nave frescoes: the Old Testament (scene 5), Isaac, Esau and Jacob.

35

1. Nave frescoes: the Old Testament (scene 6), Jacob's dream. 2. Nave frescoes: the Old Testament (scene 7), Joseph's dream and the envious brothers. 3. Nave frescoes: the Old Testament (scene 8), Joseph sold and Jacob weeping. 4. A detail of the previous scene with Joseph, his brothers and the merchants.

Page 38-39. 1. Nave frescoes: the Old Testament (scene 9), Joseph blames Benjamin.

36

37

1. Nave frescoes: the Old Testament (scene 10). Jacob blesses his sons. 2. Nave frescoes: the Old Testament (scene 14), Moses receives the ten commandments.

40

3

4

3. Nave frescoes: the Old Testament (scene 16), Joshua stops the sun. 4. Nave frescoes: the Old Testament (scene 17), Daniel in the lion's den.

Scenes from the New Testament

1. Nave frescoes: the New Testament (scene 20), annunciation and visitation. 2. A detail of the annunciation: the Virgin. 3. Nave frescoes: the New Testament (scene 21), nativity. 4. Nave frescoes: the New Testament (scene 22), the adoration of the Magi.

3

4

1. A detail of the slaughter of the innocents; Herod. 2. Nave frescoes: the New Testament (scene 23), the slaughter of the innocents and the flight into Egypt. 3. Nave frescoes: the New Testament (scene 24), the presentation of Christ in the temple.

1. Nave frescoes: the New Testament (scene 25), the baptism of Jesus. 2. Nave frescoes: the New Testament (scene 26), the Cana's wedding. 3. Nave frescoes: the New Testament (scene 27), the resurrection of the synagogue priest's daughter. 4. Nave frescoes: the New Testament (scene 28), the resurrection of the widow's son.

1

2

48

4

1. Nave frescoes: the New Testament (scene 29), Lazarus' resurrection. 2. Nave frescoes: the New Testament (scene 30), the entry into Jerusalem. 3. Nave frescoes: the New Testament (scene 31), the Last Supper. 4. A detail of the Last Supper.

49

50

1. Nave frescoes: the New Testament (scene 32), the prayer in the garden, the Judas' kiss and Christ's capture. 2. Nave frescoes: the New Testament (scene 33), the crucifixion. 3. Nave frescoes: the New Testament (scene 34), the deposition from the cross. 4. Nave frescoes: the New Testament (scene 35), the angel's apparition to the Pious Women. 5. Nave frescoes: the New Testament (scene 36), «noli me tangere» («do not touch me»).

3

4

5

1

Scenes from the Apocalypse

1. Nave frescoes: the apocalypse (scene 42), God shows the Seniors the seven sealsbook, detail. 2. Nave frescoes: the apocalypse (scene 42), the vision of the seven candlesticks. 3. Nave frescoes: the apocalypse (scene 42), God shows the Seniors the seven seals book.

2

3

53

4

5

1. Nave frescoes: the apocalypse (scene 43), the lamb of God among the evangelists'symbols. 2. Nave frescoes: the apocalypse (scene 44), the apocalypse knights. 3. Aisle frescoes: the apocalypse (scene 45), the apocalypse knights. 4. Nave frescoes: the apocalypse (scene 47), the angel. 5. Nave frescoes: the apocalypse (scene 48), the angel offers the book to St. John.

1. Nave frescoes: the apocalypse (scene 51), the church threatened by the hydra. 2. Nave frescoes: the apocalypse (scene 53), the beast with seven heads. 3. Nave frescoes: the apocalypse (scene 52), the angels fighting against the devil. 4. Nave frescoes: (scene 53 et 54), the beast with seven heads and dragons attacking the Saint Book.

3

4

1. Nave frescoes: (scenes 55-56), the son of Man reprimands the blonde prostitute. 2. The blonde prostitute, a detail of the scene 56.

4

3. Nave frescoes: the apocalypse (scenes 57-58), an arcade with the apocalypse knights and the angels. 4. Nave frescoes: the apocalypse (scene 48), the angel.

ing; in a lower position he is sitting on his throne with open arms; rows of angels, saints and blessed souls are crowding in a regular arrangement, toward him, while the damned are painted only on the two panels below to the right.

The fresco cycle on the nave and the counter-façade are attributed by critics to a time about twenty years later than that of the apse frescoes, even though some suggest Vitale da Bologna may be the deviser of the decoration plan of the whole church. At any rate, although the actual authors came undoubtedly from Bologna and were there-

1. The church, counter-façade fresco: the Last Judgement, (second half of the 14th century). 2. The Last Judgement: detail with angels and saints.

fore connected to the Maestro by the same cultural milieu, they were nonetheless independent in their lively, sometimes popular expressivity.

As mentioned above, the church was thoroughly re-frescoed in the second half of the 14th century; the decoration, which is made of figures in the church central space and apses, becomes a geometrical coating displaying false precious marbles in the aisles, where panels hint at marble inlays or contain figures of saints inside multifoiled frameworks. This decoration scheme continues unbroken on the walls also covering the original frescoes. A portion of them can be seen on the façade's side parts where the figures (dating back to about the 10th century), which surrounded the two-light windows of the original atrium, appear on the surface.

apse, demolished in the 14th century, have been found just recently and are now displayed in the right aisle.

Beside an interesting holy-water stoup, supported by telamon figures (about 12th century), a portion of the floor made of coccio pesto * which was in the church before 1026 and the remains of the

1. Aisle frescoes with fake marble geometrical decoration (second half of the 14th century). 2. A detail of the decorations of the aisles: a figure of a saint. 3. A detail of the under-arches decoration: the star with eight points with the inscription «POMPOSIA» is the symbol of the Abbey.

3

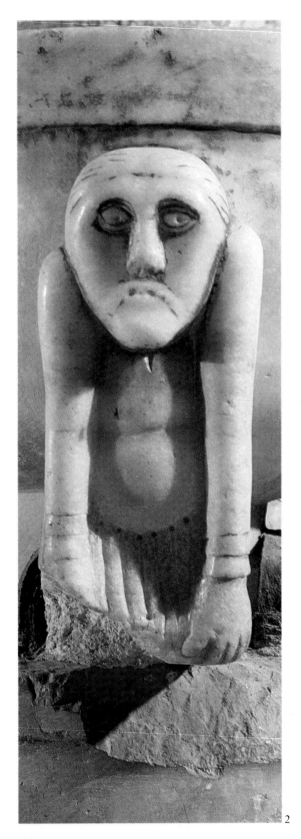

1. A romanesque holy water stoup supported by telamons. 2. Telamon, detail a romanesque holy water stoup. 3. A comprehensive view of the Abbey's former dormitory, which has become the Pomposa museum.

The museum of Pomposa

We come into the Museum through the stairs which, starting at the end of the right aisle, lead to the big hall which was originally the Abbey's dormitory.

The exhibited objects come from the church or from the destroyed parts of the group of buildings and a visit to the museum means therefore going again through the centuries-old history of Pomposa with the help of the single pieces, over a period stretching from the 6th to the 19th century.

It is a very heterogeneous collection, made of peeled-off frescoes, brickwork elements, stucco works, marbles and everyday objects, coming in most cases from systematic excavations or from accidental findings. In particular cases the objects were removed from their original position and gathered inside the Museum in order to give tourists and scholars a better opportunity to observe them.

There is no chronologically arranged path, each group of objects forming a subject of its own; however it is advisable to begin the visit from the right side of the hall following the numeration of the exhibited objects.

The group of terracotta statues (No. 1 to 6) representing the Continents comes from the garden of the farm to which Pomposa belonged after the Napoleonic suppressions: the neoclassic statues remind us of one of the worst periods in the history of Pomposa.

Architectural and decorative fragments made of brickwork, stucco and marble of different origin are displayed in three glass-cases (No. 178 to 209); among them, in No. 209, the fragment of a stucco barrier (8th-9th century) is of particular interest: it belonged to the original structure of the church.

On the wall (No. 10) is an interesting capital made of Greek marble of Byzantine art (6th century); for the typical inclination of the acanthus leaves this capital is said of the kind «with leaves stirred by the wind».

The stucco slab No. 120 is among the rarest pieces of the whole collection; it is a pluteus * which belonged once to the presbyterial enclosure

1. Terracotta statues (19th century) representing the continents (No.s 1-6). 2. A stucco slab of the presbytery enclosure (7th-8th century), (No. 120). 3. A sinopite of the Verona school (late 14th century) from the court house (No. 22).

of the church and was later used as case for the holy oils.

The frontal bas-relief decoration is divided into three parts by pilaster strips connected by small round arches; inside, the drawing with shoots branching from schematic vases and leaves in the lunettes puts the ornamentation in relation with the Byzantine art of the 7th and 8th century. On its back the central space has been chiselled while, below, strip-like shoots ending with heart-shaped leaves are still to be seen.

Of the same kind are the five pluteus fragments (No. 15) found in the church during the excavations of 1978-79 between the 11th century floor and the previous one.

No. 20 and 22 are a fresco of Veronese school removed from the Court-house and its corresponding sinopite * that may be dated to the end of the 14th century. These works begin a series of frescoes alternated, in the exhibition, with marble architectural elements dating back to different periods: among them, the fountain coming from the anterefectory (end of the 15th century) is of a certain interest.

The decoration carried out after 1350 inside the church aisles is represented by No. 26 where we can see panels of false marble framing decorative elements and the figure of a saint.

In the middle, in front of the Museum's entrance, are two big frescoes: No. 28, removed in 1963 from the left upper level of the façade, represents a battle from the Old Testament of uncertain identification; although many parts are missing the high pictorial quality and expressive skill of the unknown author belonging to the Bologna school of the middle of the 14th century are still clearly recognizable.

No. 29 is a fresco coming from the atrium, namely from the part overlooking the church entrance door; it was also painted by an artist of the Bologna school of the middle of the 14th century and represents the Virgin on her throne with Child and two angels.

The following object is a rare example of the pictorial decorations which used to adorn the church before those of the 14th century: it is the underside of the arch of the right lateral apse (9th century).

At No. 113 (No. 114 is identical but with many missing parts) the most remarkable piece is a pluteus made of Greek marble which belonged to the choir enclosure in the 11th century. The theme of intertwined bands describing two circles, the animals inside (a rampant basilisk and two drakes bound at their necks by a chain), the leaves filling up the external surfaces, all that shows the oriental inspiration of the work which was therefore attributed to skilled workers linked to Mazulo, the master of the atrium (first half of the 11th century).

A meaningful example of the frequent reuse of the material of Pomposa is the frieze fragment with a stylized owl of Byzantine inspiration (10th century) having on its back an iscription of the 14th century with the eight-pointed star, symbol of the Abbey.

No. 87 leads us to the same theme: in it we find remains of Roman inscriptions, evidently the original utilization of the block; turned into a holy-water stoup in the 8th century, it suffered another change in the 12th century when it became a ciborium *.

On the wall, on special supports, there is a rich group of Romanesque architectural elements most

---

1. A small fountain of the 15th century. 2. A fresco detached from the church (second half of the 14th century), (No. 26). 3. A fresco detached from the nave representing a battle from the Old Testament. (It belongs to the cycle of the second half of the 14th century).

2

3

na and Venice and give therefore evidence of the close relation then existing (6th century) between the northern Adriatic shore and Byzantium.

In the next four glass-cases are some everyday objects (ceramics, glass, etc.) and fragments of decorative basins of the bell tower, examples of Egyptian-Fatimid art of the 10th century (No. 173 to 176).

To end the collection are four ogival arched lintels coming from the 14th century façade of the Court-house and removed when the upper open galleries were reinstated.

of which belonged once to the destroyed cloister: bases, small columns fragments and capitals decorated with fantastic figures.

In the middle of the hall are two precious sculpture elements recently moved from the church to the museum and namely a pulvin of the second half of the 6th century, which served as a base (No. 86) and a beautiful capital used for centuries as holy-water stoup (No. 85): it is a funnel-shaped, fretworked capital of evident Byzantine inspiration having shoots interlaced with thorned leaves in the surfaces bordered by wave-like bands.

Pieces almost identical with this one can be found in Parenzo: they have lots of stylistic features in common with other objects from Raven-

1. A marble pluteus representing a basilisk and dragons (first half of the 11th century), (No. 113). 2. A fragment of a frieze with a griffin (end of the 10th century). On the back there is an inscription with the Pomposa mark (No. 112). 3. A group of architectural marbles, coming from the demolished cloister. 4. A ciborium of the 12th century, made out of a reused block with an inscription later become a holy-water stoup (7th century). (No. 87). 5. A big byzantine capital (6th century) used as holy-water stoup (No. 85).

3

4

5

1-2. Domestic pottery used in the Abbey (about 14th-16th century). 2. A jug with an eight-pointed star, the symbol of the Abbey (14th century).

3

1. Pomposa objects: notice the processional cross of the 16th century (No. 165) and the oriental ceramic fragments coming from the decorative basins of the tower of the bell (10th-11th century). 2. Jugs and plates (from the 14th to 16th century). 3. A marble sun-dial of the 16th century. 4. A cloister with well-curb and capitular hall façade.

The capitular hall

On leaving the church and after noticing the angular pillars marking the shape of the destroyed cloister (12th century), we come into the Capitular hall which is of remarkable importance because of the frescoes covering its walls: in front of the entrance, between the windows, are displayed a Crucifixion and, on both its sides, the figures of St. Peter and St. Paul inside two niches; on the lateral walls are St. Benedict and St. Guido, the saints of Pomposa, in niches similar to the previous ones. These are followed, on each wall, by panels with Gothic two-light windows inside which prophets are painted monochromo. The upper panels and bands, as well as the entrance wall, bear geometrical decorations.

The hall is of the highest interest because of its decorative scheme, enhanced by the strong plasticity of the architectural structures as well as by the magnificence of the figures. Critics, however, do not wholly agree about the authorship even if it seems likely that these frescoes were painted by an artist who knew the works of Giotto very well, if not by Giotto himself, as it was suggested in the past.

Although the presence of Giotto in Pomposa and in Ferrara is to be excluded, it seems plausible that the Maestro, who worked in Padua in 1305-1306, may have influenced the unknown author of the Capitular hall; moreover, the hall's frescoes rather than to a workshop of pupils seem to be attributable to the creative work of only one mind, an artist who gave Pomposa one of the highest examples of Po-Valley painting of the early 14th century.

Remarkable is also the wooden ceiling with carved corbels and painted bands.

*1. Capitular hall, crucifixion fresco: the painter was influenced
by Giotto, (beginning of the 14th century). 2. The crucifixion,
a detail of figures of soldiers.*

Pages 78-79. Right wall of the capitular hall: prophets' fresco; Moses and David, Jeremiah and Isaiah. The painter was influenced by Giotto (beginning of the 16th century).

S · YSAIA · PHA   S · IHEREMIA · PHA

1

1. Right wall of the capitular hall: a detail of St. Guido. The painter shows Giotto influences (beginning of the 14th century). 2. Left wall of the capitular hall: a detail of St. Benedict. The painter is from the Giotto school (beginning of the 14th century).

81

The refectory

Between 1316 and 1320 the friars of Pomposa commissioned the new frescoes of the Refectory which thus covered the old ones.

On the end wall there is the most celebrated fresco of the big 14th century Pomposa cycle. It is divided into three parts by small spiral columns and has in its middle, in the foreground, a Deesis in which the blessing Redeemer is between the Virgin and St. John the Baptist: on both sides of them are two Pomposa saints, St. Benedict and St. Guido. The painting on the left represents the Last Supper, while that on the right shows a major event of the Monastery's life: Abbot St. Guido performs the miracle of the turning of water into wine in presence of Gebeardo, the bishop of Ravenna.

The fresco, although attributed in the past to Pietro da Rimini who, however, at the time the fresco was painted, had already achieved a more complex maturity of style and space, is to be attributed to artists of the Rimini-school of the 14th century.

Several critics have drawn attention to some archaic features of the work and to the unadornedness of the scenes (the steadiness of the Deesis, the scheme of the Last Supper and of St. Guido's miracle, considered «almost from the 13th century» by Volpe) together with a flat painting where the light and shade seem mere technique. However, critics agree that these frescoes are the unequalled greatest in Pomposa.

On the other walls of the Refectory we can see the sinopite of the main fresco: the painting was removed from the wall for preservation reasons and therefore detached from its sinopite. Still recognizable, although only in fragments, are a Prayer in the Garden, whose painting date (1318)

---

1. A comprehensive view of the refectory. 2. The refectory: the Last Supper fresco, the Deesis, the miracle of St. Guido (1316-1328).

was found under it during a restoration in 1964, as well as other frescoes representing events of monastic life.

On the wall opposite the main frescoes is an architectural decoration having a tympanum, that may be dated to the 16th century.

1. The Deesis; beside the blessing Christ there are the Virgin Mary and St. John the Baptist. On the two sides there are St. Benedict and St. Guido. 2. The Deesis, a detail of the Virgin Mary. 3. The Last Supper. 4. The Last Supper, detail. 5. The Last Supper, detail.

2

5

1. The miracle of St. Guido: making the by-standers astonished and the friars delighted, St. Guido turns water into wine in the presence of St. Gebeardo. 2. The miracle of St. Guido, detail. 3-4. The refectory, a sinopite of the fresco on the end wall.

1. The refectory: the main hall; in the background architectural decoration of the 15th century. 2. The angular pillar of the cloister (11th century). 3. The court-house seen from the cloister. 4. A cloister well-curb (15th century).

The court-house

As mentioned in the historical background, because of a particular form of feudal organization with direct jurisdiction over his possessions, the Abbot of Pomposa was also charged with the administration of justice over the surrounding territory.

This civil function was performed in the Court-house, most probably built under St. Guido or, in any way, before the 12th century.

Main feature of the building is the high simplicity of its structure, which however was very much impoverished in our century by an almost complete reconstruction.

The façade, still the original one, has a double open gallery which shows a vague influence from the urban architecture of Venice, though the forms displayed here retain a character of their own.

A thorough examination reveals a marked difference between the vertical props of the ground floor and those of the upper floor: the latter were in fact added a few decades ago when, during an imperfect restoration, it was thought to reinstate the open gallery on the first floor. The result was an upsetting of the shape the façade had taken on in 1396 when Abbot Bonaccorso had let the original gallery be closed up by a continuous wall broken only by five ogival windows.

Therefore only the architectural elements on the ground floor were built during the construction of the House, but here, rather than elsewhere in the Abbey, are columns and capitals of a great variety of sizes and forms which again are spoil pieces from the region of Ravenna.

Originally, the Court-house façade was also adorned with the maiolica basin decoration schemes seen in the atrium, but unfortunately they are now totally lost.

3

*1. Façade of the court-
house. 2. The court-
house, a foreshortening of
the front. 3. A detail of
the lower loggia (open-
sided gallery).*

91

1. The lower ambulatory. 2. The memorial stone of abbot Bonaccorso (1396). It was placed on the courthouse façade during rebuilding works. 3. A detail of the lower loggia: particularly interesting is the marked difference among spoil capitals, columns and bases.

Pomposian poem by Giovanni Pascoli

Years now, they were a thousand, that sowing, pastures and villas. I had and gathered honey and wine, and flaxen sheaves, pregnant flocks in sheepfolds, fat, farmyard fowl in courtyards; that the lowing kine foretold luminous dawns, that all the petals, by my hand tended, flowered the land.
And that I, Pomposia, raised my saint and unremitting song: O Lord! Send forth from the furrows manifold fruit to the ploughman; to all, sweet life, and death borne lightly: halcyon sun as our torch, labour as token of peace.
Thus, afterwards the time came when from Lethean sleep taken I fell. The good ploughing on mother land ceased, and when even the rakes were lost, I was left alone under the stars.
The nearby Bora and, afar, the raging, shattering furies of the waves screamed me wretched.
And of the many monks who lie interred in hallow'd ground, tempestuous nights heard the lugubrious, melancholy lament.
Now at last the marsh completes its ancient rites, and grass and bracken clad its banks.
Once more astonished, I feel again the life flowing inside me. J hear a breeze from ancient times caress the happy harvest and my monk Guido chant with his devoted choir.

94

Glossary

Abbey: architectural group composed of many buildings each one used with a different function (church, capitular hall, refectory, library, etc.). In the Abbey religious live as a community led by an abbot.

Apse: terminal part of the basilica, composed of a semi-circular wall on which the apse basin rests.

Atrium (entrance hall): porch entrance serving as a filter between the outside and the interior of the building.

Basilica: in Christian architecture the word means a church characterized by a longitudinal plan, in opposition to the central plan church.

Basin: Small dome placed in the upper part of the apse, shaped as the fourth part of a sphere.

Choir: enclosure near the main altar: religious gathered there to sing liturgies separated from the rest of the congregation.

Ciborium: tabernacle, small shrine placed on the altar to keep the eucharistical species.

Cloister: yard enclosed by an arcade, situated usually between the church and the other monastery buildings.

Coccio pesto: mixture of different grains, composed of pounded laterite and mortar lime: it was mainly used as mortar in damp environments, or as beaten layer for making floors.

Crypt: hall or group of rooms placed underground, usually under the church presbyterial area.

Cuspide (Cusp): triangular architectural end.

Fatimite: art of the Fatimite's age: a dynasty of Muslim califs who ruled over the northern Africa from 969 to 1171.

Fresco: «a fresco» wall painting: colours are applied straightly onto a moist plaster surface of sand and lime. The colour is allowed to dry on the surface and to fix on it, becoming incorporated into the plaster support.

Lesena (pilaster strip): semi-pilaster or semi-column leaning against a wall to give decorative rhythm to its surface.

Monofora (not mullioned window): one-light window generally ending with an arch.

Mosaic: walls and pavements decorating technique. It is composed of «tesserae» (small coloured bits of stone and/or glass mixture) applied to a specially pre-arranged wall surface.

Mullioned window: window divided into two equal parts by a vertical stone (small column or pilaster).

Nave: part of internal space resulting from the lengthwise division of a rectangular hall: churches with a basilical plan have three or five naves.

Pluteus: full slab decorated with reliefs, serving as an enclosure of the choir or the presbytery, just like the transenna.

Presbytery: part of the church reserved for the clergy, placed in the end portion of the nave; usually it is higher than the floor to make the course of the holy ceremonies visible.

Pulvin: it is an architectural element connecting capital to arch, typical of the byzantine art.

Quadrifora (four-light window): window divided into four equal parts by vertical elements.

Sinopite: Preliminary sketch of a fresco or a mosaic, made with earth of sinope, natural red earth. The word comes from the town of Sinope, on the Black Sea, where the earth was digged out.

Spoil: the word refers to the habit of collecting old architectural elements from their original site to reuse them in other edifices as building or decorative materials.

Stucco: mixture of building materials used for decorating purposes since ancient times. It is composed of fine-grained sand and marble powder mixed together with slaked lime (but its composition changed according to ages and places).

Tarsia: decorating technique based on the inlaid work done on a drawing with different materials: the marble tarsia, used on walls and floors since the greek classic age, knew a large diffusion in the byzantine, paleochristian and romanesque art.

Transenna: pierced slab used as enclosure of a window or a surrounded site (see pluteus).

Trifora (three-light window): window divided in three equal parts by vertical elements.

Triumphal arch: partition-wall of the nave and the presbytery: the apse opens onto this wall.

List of contents

Distribuzione esclusiva
LANZAadg

LANZA A.D.G. di Lanza Barbara & C. snc
Via L. Bottoni, 34
44038 Ponte Lagoscuro - Ferrara
Tel. 0532/464717 - 463985 - Fax 0532/796394
e-mail: info@puntoedicola.com

Grafica e impaginazione: Federico Frassinetti
Fotografie: Ascanio Ascani - Misano (Forlì) - Federico Fressinetti

edizioni ITALCARDS
Modena - Italy